NOV 0 2 2005

ELECTRICITY

Please visit our web site at: **www.garethstevens.com**
For a free color catalog describing Gareth Stevens Publishing's list of high-quality books and multimedia programs, call 1-800-542-2595 (USA) or 1-800-387-3178 (Canada). Gareth Stevens Publishing's fax: (414) 332-3567.

Library of Congress Cataloging-in-Publication Data

Electricity.—North American ed.
        p. cm. — (Discovery Channel school science: physical science)
    "First published in 1999 as Shock: the electricity files by Discovery Enterprises, LLC, Bethesda, Maryland" — T.p. verso.
    Summary: Presents information and instructions for activities related to principles of electricity and their manifestations in daily life.
    ISBN 0-8368-3356-2 (lib. bdg.)
    1. Electricity—Juvenile literature. [1. Electricity.] I. Title. II. Series.
QC527.2.E4414   2003
537—dc21   2002030528

This edition first published in 2003 by
Gareth Stevens Publishing
A World Almanac Education Group Company
330 West Olive Street, Suite 100
Milwaukee, WI 53212 USA

This U.S. edition © 2003 by Gareth Stevens, Inc. First published in 1999 as *Shock: The Electricity Files* by Discovery Enterprises, LLC, Bethesda, Maryland. © 1999 by Discovery Communications, Inc.

Further resources for students and educators available at www.discoveryschool.com

Designed by Bill SMITH STUDIO
Creative Director: Ron Leighton
Design: Eric Hoffsten, Jay Jaffe, Brian Kobberger, Nick Stone, Sonia Gauba
Production Directors: Peter Lindstrom, Paula Radding
Photo Editor: Justine Price
Art Buyer: Lillie Caporlingua
Print consulting by Debbie Honig, Active Concepts
Gareth Stevens Editor: Betsy Rasmussen
Gareth Stevens Art Director: Tammy Gruenewald

Printed in the United States of America

1 2 3 4 5 6 7 8 9 07 06 05 04 03

Writers: Richie Chevat, Jackie Ball

Content Reviewer: Stephen M. Tomecek

Copy Editor: Joellyn M. Ausanka

Photographs: Cover, © Frank Saragnese/FPG; pp. 12-13, telephone, light bulb, iron, CORBIS/Bettmann; p. 22, Electric eel © Zig Leszczynski/Animals Animals/Earth Scenes; Blue Shark, CORBIS/Amos Nachoum; p. 23, Atlantic manta ray, CORBIS/Robert Yin; Catfish on Lake Mead, CORBIS/Richard Cummins; pp. 26-27, New York City skyline and Brooklyn Bridge, CORBIS/Bettmann.

Illustrations: pp. 4-5, Steve Gray; pp. 8-9, 10-11, Ben Franklin engraving, lightning cloud, voltaic pile and versorium, Alexis Seabrook; p. 12, telegraph operator, CORBIS/Bettmann; pp. 20-21, 24-25, Curious Circuit and You're Wired, Richard Kolding.

Acknowledgements: pp. 14-15, Franklin Jehl's reminiscences, from Menlo Park Reminiscences, Volume One, the Edison Institute, Dearborn, Michigan, 1937; p. 30, from the Papers of Thomas Edison, © 1989 Johns Hopkins University Press; p. 26, excerpt from "A View From Here" LIFE 11/19/65. Loudon Wainwright/LIFE Magazine, © Time Inc.; p. 27, 1965 blackout account, Copyright © 1998 The Blackout Education Project. Sloan.stanford.edu/Blackout/home.html

All Charged Up

We call it simply "power." Electricity is one of the most powerful forces in nature—and one of the most mysterious. It's as ordinary as your socks sticking together in the dryer and as extraordinary as the sight of jagged bolts of lightning ripping through thunderclouds. It cooks your toast, runs your computer, and powers your heart itself. No wonder people have worked so hard to understand electricity and harness its power. Discovery Channel's presentation of *ELECTRICITY* gives YOU the power to see this amazing force up close—in all its shocking forms.

ELECTRICITY

Why doesn't this worker get shocked? See page 28.

Final Project

Z-Z-Z-Zap!

It's late at night. The house is dark and still—or so you think. But all around you, trillions and trillions of tiny particles are flying in tiny circles. You can't see them, but they're there—in your walls, your ceilings, your hat, and the old pizza box under your bed. They're even . . . inside you. They zoom around the core of every atom of everything in the world, like miniature planets circling suns. They're electrons. When they're pushed or disturbed out of those orbits, they may start to flow in one direction. If these electrons flow through wires from a power plant to your house, it means just one thing: electricity. Here comes the juice.

ATOM—The smallest unit into which matter can be divided without losing its unique properties.
Nucleus: The core of an atom, containing protons, parts with a positive charge, and neutrons, parts with no electric charge.
Electrons: Parts of an atom that have a negative electric charge.

CONDUCTOR—A material through which electricity can flow easily, such as copper.

INSULATOR—A material through which electricity cannot flow easily, such as rubber.

CIRCUIT—A closed loop of wires or other conductors.

CURRENT—The flow of electrons.

POWER PLANT—Where electricity is made or generated.

STEP-UP TRANSFORMER—Station between the power plant and your house that increases the flow of electrons.

STEP-DOWN TRANSFORMER—Station between the power lines coming from the power plant and the wires going to your house. They decrease the flow of electrons.

SWITCH—A device that closes and opens a circuit, breaking the flow or allowing the flow of electrons.

CIRCUIT BREAKER—A device that switches off electricity if too much current is flowing through the wires.

negative attitude

But wait a minute. All those lights and electric things in your room didn't just happen overnight. Neither did the elaborate system of getting electricity to your house. First, people had to figure out what this mysterious force was. Then they had to know how to make it work and what it might do. How **DOES** it work? Let's go to the source.

Q: So you're an electron. Can you describe your average day for us?
A: Sure, but you'll excuse me if I don't stop and chat. Gotta keep moving. Round and round, round and round, you know the drill. I guess someone's gotta do it, but most of the time I feel as if I'm getting nowhere.

Q: You sound kind of negative.
A: Well, what do you expect from an electron? I AM negative. All electrons are. We're negatively charged. What do you think this little minus sign means?

Q: Oh, yeah, there it is. Well, those protons over there are wearing little plus signs, so they must be positive. Would you rather be a proton?
A: No way! Those poor guys, trapped inside that nucleus night and day. How they keep a positive charge is beyond me. At least I get to run around out here. Get some exercise. And sometimes—I get to escape.

Q: What do you mean?
A: See, most of the time atoms are very well balanced. They have the exact same number of electrons as protons. Same number of negatives as positives. And you know what that means: balance. Order.

Q: What about the neutrons in the nucleus?
A: Them? Oh, they don't count. They have no charge. Zip. They're real zeroes. Talk about boring!

Q: I suppose. Anyway, what do you mean, "most of the time" atoms are well balanced?

A: Every once in awhile, there's a little push. A jolt. A disturbance.

Q: What kind of disturbance?
A: Well, sometimes we jump to other kinds of atoms—but that's chemistry! Sometimes the disturbance could be as simple as friction—two objects rubbing against each other. Doesn't take much to upset some of us electrons. We're kind of edgy. Maybe it comes from spending so much time in orbit, out here on the edge. Anyway, we get transferred. Booted out of our orbits. Painful! We go flying off the first object and clump up on the second in a big heap. Then we stand still. That's why this kind of electricity is called static electricity. Static means standing still. But watch out. We're still charged up. We still have the power.

Q: The power to do what?
A: To make a spark, like when you shuffle across a wool rug and touch a metal doorknob. That's because electrons have been

transferred from the wool rug to you. Electrons accumulate on you. The charge builds up on your hand and jumps off to the nearest conductor, which is the doorknob. Now the doorknob is negatively charged. It has too many electrons.

Q: **What about the wool?**
A: It has too many protons. It's positively charged. Same thing happens with clothes out of a dryer. Notice how they cling together? The heat and motion of the dryer has disturbed electrons, so they've jumped from your socks to your T-shirt. Your socks have a positive charge. Your T-shirt has a negative one. Try to pull them apart and—zap! Gotcha! Static electricity.

Q: **But why do positively charged and negatively charged things stick together?**
A: Because they have a force that makes them push and pull at each other. The atoms want to get back into balance! The particles miss each other. It's a natural thing. Positives and negatives are attracted to each other. Ever hear the expression "opposites attract"?

Q: **Sure. But I thought that had to do with magnets.**
A: Well . . . ta-da! Get ready for a REAL shock! Electricity and magnetism are displays of the same force. They're both about positives and negatives. Opposite things attracting. Like things repelling each other. Push, pull. Push, pull. It makes the world work. But ask me if all electricity is made by friction. Go ahead, ask me. Come on.

Q: **OK. Is all electricity made by friction?**

A: I'm so glad you asked! Nope, no, and nah.

Q: **You're sounding negative again.**
A: I told you, I can't help it. But static electricity is just one kind of electricity. It's electricity at rest. The other kind is current electricity. That's electricity in motion, the kind that's a steady flow of electrons through certain things.

Q: **Only through certain things?**
A: Right. Materials called conductors. Copper and other metals. And water. Electricity moves through wet things faster than dry ones. See, conductors have electrons that free up easily. They get knocked out of orbit, and then what do you think happens?

Q: **What?**
A: Well, they need a home. So they hook up with another atom. But that knocks off the electron that was already there! It's like when you're in line at the movies, and the kid behind you gives you a shove. Well, you don't just stand there. You push the kid in front of you. She bumps into the one in front of her, and the bumps move down the line. That's what current electricity is like.

Q: **Hey, no shoving please. What things can't electricity flow through easily? And are they more polite?**

A: The ones called insulators. Their electrons are held tightly in place. They wouldn't budge if you paid them. Stuff like rubber and plastic are insulators. Glass is good too. You gotta remember that electrons follow the path of least resistance. If they can't get in somewhere easily, they'll get in somewhere else.

Q: **So that's why wires are wrapped in plastic.**
A: You got it. Plastic doesn't let in any outside electrons. That door is locked. No vacancy. Keep out.

Q: **One last question: Do you prefer being part of static electricity or current?**
A: Usually it's more fun to flow. Just jumping from T-shirts to dish towels isn't all that much fun. People hardly notice. But there's a kind of static electricity that's hard not to notice.

Q: **What is it?**
A: Here's a hint: Ka-boom! Crackle! Snap!

Q: **Lightning, right?**
A: Bingo! That's when static electricity gets to put on a show. That's when we heat up—six times hotter than the surface of the sun. And the first guy who figured out that lightning is electricity? He is my hero. He made me famous!

Activity

ARE YOU POSITIVE? Inflate two balloons and tie strings to them. Now tie the balloons to a hanger in a place where they can hang freely. What happens? Rub each balloon with a piece of wool or fur. Now what happens? Last, put your hand between the two balloons. Write down all your observations and try to draw conclusions about what's happening.

Go Fly a Kite

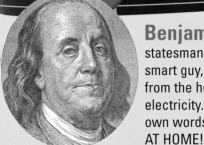

Benjamin Franklin (1706-1790), statesman, inventor, and a very curious and smart guy, is said to have "snatched electricity from the heavens" by proving lightning was electricity. Here's his famous experiment, in his own words. But remember—DON'T TRY THIS AT HOME!

What Franklin Used

- **Silk fabric**
- **Kite with metal point at top**
- **Twine** (When wet, the twine acted as a conductor of electricity)
- **Silk ribbon at bottom** (Franklin stood under a shelter to keep himself and the ribbon dry so it would not conduct electricity)
- **Metal key**

Philadelphia, PA, 1752

"The Kite is to be raised, when a Thunder Gust appears to be comeing on (which is very frequent in this country) & The Person who holds the String must stand within a Door, or Window, or under some cover, so that the Silk Ribbon may not be Wet; & care must be taken that the Twine does not touch the Frame of the Door or Window. As soone as any of the thunder Clouds come over the Kite, the pointed wire will draw the Electric Fire from them, & the Kite, with all the Twine, will be Electrified and the loose filaments of the Twine will stand out every way and be attracted by an approaching finger.

"When the Rain has Wett the Kite and Twine, so that it can conduct the Electric Fire freely, you will find it stream out plentifully from the Key on the approach of your knuckle."

Luckily, Franklin's kite was not actually hit by a bolt of lightning. If it had been, he would probably have been killed. But the electrified air carried enough current to make its point. When he touched the key with his knuckle, he was zapped with a strong spark. Painful, but it proved that lightning was electricity—static electricity.

8

Lightning? Frightening!

⚡ Lightning is the result of giant electrical charges that build up in thunderclouds. The flow of air and water in the clouds creates an imbalance in electrons within the cloud and between the cloud and the ground.

⚡ More people are killed every year by lightning than by tornadoes and hurricanes combined.

⚡ If you are caught outside in a thunderstorm and can't get in a building, do not stand under a tree. Go into a ditch and lie down. Above all—do not fly a kite!

Activity

PLAYING IT SAFER: Franklin's experiment with the kite was really very dangerous. A year later, a scientist in France who tried the same experiment was killed by lightning. Prepare a lightning facts brochure. Illustrate it with helpful drawings to show the hazards of lightning. Include the following facts in the brochures: cloud formation; evolution of a lightning bolt and electrical charges; lightning production; temperature of a lightning bolt; lightning conduction; thunder; lightning research; lightning safety.

BATTERIES

Benjamin Franklin discovered that lightning was static electricity, but he wasn't the first to discover static electricity itself. People had been experimenting with this force for hundreds of years.

Ancient Greece, about 600 B.C.

Thales of Miletus and other Greek scientists conduct some of the earliest experiments with electricity. They find that if a piece of amber—fossilized tree sap—is rubbed with fur or cloth, it will attract lightweight objects such as feathers. They don't know why it happens, but their work is monumentally important to what will come later. In fact, the word electricity comes from the Greek word *elektron*, which means amber.

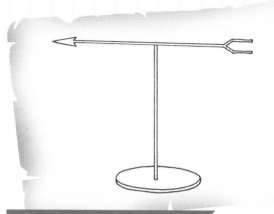

London, England, 1600

William Gilbert, a doctor to Queen Elizabeth I, uses the word *electricity* for the first time, after performing experiments in which he rubs objects on glass tubes to make static electricity. Later, Gilbert invents the first device to detect electric charges, called the versorium. It looks like a small weather vane with a wire pointer that swings toward objects with an electric charge.

The problem with static electricity is that it only has limited uses. It comes and goes in flashes of lightning and sparks. Interesting, but not especially helpful. It takes a dead frog to make the next leap—to electricity that can be stored and released gradually.

INCLUDED

Luigi Galvani, a professor of anatomy at the Academy of Science, studies frogs. He notices that sparks from a machine in his lab can make the legs of a dead frog twitch. He performs other experiments in which he makes the frog's leg jump by touching it with different pieces of metal while it lies on a metal table. Galvani concludes (wrongly) that electricity from the leg itself is making it move.

But fellow scientist Allesandro Volta has another idea. He thinks (correctly) that the electricity comes from the different metals touching the frog. He thinks that the wet frog leg is only a conductor of electricity. Volta uses his discovery to invent the first battery in 1800.

Volta announces that he's come up with a way to produce electricity continuously, not just in isolated sparks. His invention becomes known as the voltaic pile (right). But it's really the first battery.

What is a battery, anyway? It is a storage place for certain chemicals that can release an electric charge that can flow in an electric current.

Batteries work by chemical reactions. In the first battery, disks of zinc, pasteboard soaked with a salt solution or vinegar, and copper were put together in a kind of sandwich. Electrons flowed from the copper to the zinc through the solution, creating an electric current. Batteries today may use different chemicals, but they work in basically the same way.

Activity

LEMON-AID: Make your own battery out of a lemon. Really. Insert one strip of copper and one strip of zinc deeply into a lemon, making sure the strips don't touch. Use a voltmeter to measure the voltage between the two strips. It should be about one volt. Electrons flow through the acidic lemon juice.

THAT'S

Once scientists had a place to store an electrical charge—a battery—they could make more and more inventions. The world started moving faster and faster—and getting smaller and smaller.

| 1821 | 1837 | 1844 | 1840s–1879 | 1876 |

ELECTRIC MOTOR

Drawing on the work of Danish scientist Hans Christian Oersted, who showed that electricity and magnets are parts of the same force, Michael Faraday and Joseph Henry, working independently, build the first electric motor. Faraday's motor, like all the electrical inventions that would follow until the end of the century, runs on direct current, the kind of current that comes from batteries.

AMERICAN TELEGRAPH

The first practical telegraph is invented by William Cooke and Charles Wheatstone. But their system needs five wires to work. In 1840, American Samuel Morse, with the help of others, demonstrates a simple code that can be sent on one wire.

ARC LIGHT

The first electric light sparkles on the Place de la Concorde, a major avenue in Paris. But something is missing: a light bulb. That's because it's an arc light, simply a spark of electricity jumping between two pieces of carbon. Within 15 to 20 years, arc lights will be used for street lighting in New York, Cleveland, and many other cities around the world.

LIGHT BULB (IN PROGRESS)

Arc lamps have built-in problems. They're noisy, and their light is too glaring for home use. Inventors spend the next few decades working on the light bulb, a glass bulb with a thread or wire called a filament inside it. One big problem: air in the bulb. Without a vacuum—the absence of air—the glowing thread or filament would quickly burn out.

TELEPHONE

Alexander Graham Bell invents the telephone while working on ways to improve the telegraph. The first phone call happens by mistake, when Bell spills some battery acid on himself and yells to his assistant, "Watson! Come here, I want you!" His assistant hears him over the phone.

A SWITCH!

TELEPHONE, ELECTRIC PEN, ELECTRIC LIGHT BULB

Thomas Alva Edison, American technological genius, sets up the world's first industrial research laboratory. He secures patents for thousands of inventions, including the telephone (an improved version of Bell's), the electric pen, and, after fourteen months of searching for the right filament, the electric light bulb.

HOUSEHOLD APPLIANCES

The electric iron introduces a new era of amazing devices to make household chores easier. The iron hisses and sputters when it's plugged in because of the electric spark inside. The next twenty years will see the introduction of the electric vacuum cleaner and the electric stove, among other things.

TESLA COIL

Serbian immigrant Nikola Tesla introduces the idea of alternating current and invents the Tesla coil. Alternating current is how our homes and buildings are powered today. Thomas Edison, heavily invested in direct current power plants, tries to turn the public against "AC."

ALTERNATING CURRENT

Tesla sells patents for more than one hundred electrical inventions, including the first automobile speedometer, to George Westinghouse. This helps establish the Westinghouse Company as a world leader in the electrical industry. Tesla also designs a wireless broadcasting system designed to transmit voices, pictures, and electricity. It is such a revolutionary idea that people think he is insane.

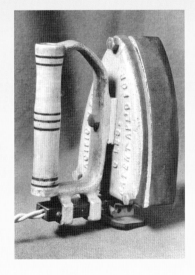

Activity

WHO'S YOUR HERO? **Thomas Edison and Nikola Tesla both made enormous contributions in the field of electricity. Do some research. List the inventions they patented and study their lives. Then have a class debate about whose contribution was greater.**

Driving Darkness Away

The hunt for the right filament was long and tiring, as Francis Jehl, one of Edison's assistants, recalled years later:

Many materials which at first seemed promising fell down under later tests and had to be laid aside. Every experiment was recorded methodically in the notebooks. In many there was simply the name of the fiber and after it the initials "T.A.," meaning "Try Again."

Threads of cotton, flax, jute silks, cords, manila hemp and even hard woods were tried. . . . Chinese and Italian raw silk both boiled out and otherwise treated were among those used. Others included horsehair, fish linen, teak, spruce, boxwood, vulcanized rubber, cork, celluloid, grass fibres from everywhere, linen twine, tar paper, wrapping paper, cardboard, tissue paper, parchment, holly wood, absorbent cotton, rattan, California redwood, raw jute fiber, corn silk, and New Zealand flax.

The most interesting material of all . . . was the hair from the luxurious beards of men about the laboratory. . . . Both burned out with considerable rapidity.

On October 21, 1879, Edison made a bulb that did not burn out. Its filament was of carbonized cotton sewing thread, and Edison and Jehl sat up all night watching it shine. In Edison's words:

We sat and looked and the lamp continued to burn. None of us could go to bed, and there was no sleep for any of us for forty hours. We sat and just watched it with anxiety growing into elation. It lasted about forty-five hours, and then I said, "If it will burn that number of hours now, I know I can make it burn a hundred."

Reporters described the electric light bulb as "a veritable Aladdin's lamp . . . a little globe of sunshine." The first public demonstration of electric light took place soon afterwards.

Edison's laboratory was tonight thrown open to the general public for the inspection of his electric light. Extra trains were run from east and west, and notwithstanding the stormy weather, hundreds of persons availed themselves of the privilege. The laboratory was brilliantly illuminated with twenty-five electric lamps, the office and counting room with eight, and twenty others were distributed in the street leading to the depot and in some of the adjoining houses. The entire system was explained in detail by Edison and his assistants, and the light was subjected to a variety of tests.

[One test was] turning the electric current on and off on one of the lamps with great rapidity and as many times as it was calculated the light would be turned on and off in actual household illuminations in a period of thirty years, and no perceptible variation either in the brilliancy, steadiness or durability of the lamp occurred.

New York City, 1882

Thomas Edison's pet project, the Pearl Street Central Power Station, is completed. It makes New York the first of the world's great cities to be electrically lit. Edison is hailed as a genius, and the coming of electric light is widely seen as a way of banishing the fear and superstition that darkness has bred. German historian Emil Ludwig said that the electric light bulb meant fire had been discovered for the second time, "delivering mankind from the curse of night."

Activity

LIGHT FIGHT: There's no doubt that Thomas Edison was an important inventor, but was he really the inventor of the light bulb? A scientist named Joseph Swan worked on the filament problem for twenty years in England and also came up with the idea of a carbon coating. He patented his own version of the electric light in 1880. Do some more research, and then have a class debate.

ALMANAC Watt's What?

We measure electricity in watts, volts, amperes (or amps) and ohms.

Volts indicate the strength or "pressure" of an electric current.

Amps indicate how many electrons flow past a specific point in a circuit in a given length of time.

Watts indicate the total electrical energy being used. Volts multiplied by amps equals watts.

Here's another way of looking at it. The number of electrons moving through a circuit (amps) and the pressure those electrons are under (volts) tell you how much power the electricity has (watts).

Here's a formula to remember:
Volts × Amps = Watts

Ohms indicate the resistance to electron flow in the circuit.

RE-VOLT-ING!

Lightning strikes discharge 100 million volts of electricity.

Taking off a sweater has the potential to generate 30,000 volts.

Combing your hair has the potential to generate 10,000 volts.

Walking on a carpet has the potential to generate 3,000 volts.

Putting on a coat has the potential to generate 1,000 volts.

Why don't these everyday activities harm us? Because except for lightning, the amperage, and hence the power generated, is very small.

How many watts do we use?

A single light bulb might use 60 watts of power. Most household circuits in the United States carry 110 volts and 15 amps. When you do the math, you'll see that a single circuit can handle about 1,650 watts at one time. In other words, enough to light 27 60-watt bulbs.

A **kilowatt** is just what it sounds like: 1,000 watts. If you look on your home's electricity bill, you'll see that it is measured in kilowatt-hours. A kilowatt-hour is one kilowatt of electricity used for one hour. An average house in the United States might use a few hundred kilowatt-hours a month.

That's a Lotta Light!

How much electricity does the world use in a year? Try twelve trillion, two hundred and sixty billion, one hundred million kilowatt-hours. That's the actual figure from 1997. How was that usage divided up around the world? Look at the chart below.

Who's Got the Power?

Region	0 kilowatt-hours	1 billion kilowatt-hours	2 billion kilowatt-hours	3 billion kilowatt-hours
North America	████████████████████████████			
Central and South America	███████			
Western Europe	██████████			
Eastern Europe and the former USSR	█████████████			
Middle East	█████			
Africa	█████			
Far East	██████████████████████			

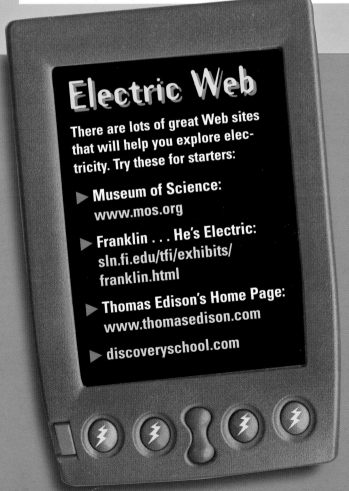

Electric Web

There are lots of great Web sites that will help you explore electricity. Try these for starters:

► **Museum of Science:** www.mos.org

► **Franklin . . . He's Electric:** sln.fi.edu/tfi/exhibits/franklin.html

► **Thomas Edison's Home Page:** www.thomasedison.com

► discoveryschool.com

Activities

THE TINE OF YOUR LIFE: Place two metal forks (tines down) several inches apart in a large glass mixing bowl of water, leaving a small portion of each fork handle exposed. Secure the forks to the side of the bowl with duct tape. Using a voltmeter, measure the voltage between the two forks. Add three tablespoons of salt to the water and measure again. Was there a difference in the voltage measurements? What could account for a difference? Repeat the activity by replacing one fork with aluminum foil or other metals.

THE NAME GAME: Which electrical terms come from scientists who advanced our knowledge of electricity? Invent terms after scientists whose names have not been used.

Power Trips

ICELAND— Geothermal energy, which comes from hot water underneath the ground, is largely used.

CALIFORNIA—Solar thermal plants throughout the state use heat from the Sun to boil water, creating steam that goes through the turbines.

NORTH AMERICA

ENGLAND—One company, British Energy, produces one-fifth of the country's electricity. It operates eight nuclear power stations.

EUROPE

NEW YORK STATE— Niagara Falls is a hydroelectric plant designed by Nikola Tesla.

NEVADA-ARIZONA BORDER—Hoover Dam, a hydroelectric power plant, serves one million people.

This map shows worldwide electrical usage. The lightning bolts pinpoint ten powerful places.

Electricity can be made by burning coal or oil, or with windmills, solar panels, dams, or nuclear power. But whatever fuel or energy is being used, almost all of the electricity in the world relies on electromagnetic generators. An electromagnetic generator does just what it sounds like: it uses magnetism to capture the energy of water, wind, Sun, or fuel to make electricity.

We already know that magnetism and electricity are parts of the same force. A current of electricity can create a magnetic field, and a magnetic field can create a current of electricity.

Every power plant has a generator. Generators contain large spinning magnets in coils of wire. As the magnets turn, they create an electric current in the wire. The magnets, which are called turbines, can be turned by steam, water pressure, or wind power.

SOUTH AMERICA

CHERNOBYL, UKRAINE— Chernobyl nuclear power plant was the site of an accident on April 26, 1986, at 1:23 AM. The people of Chernobyl were exposed to radioactivity 100 times greater than the Hiroshima bomb.

ASIA

CHINA'S YANGTZE RIVER—Three Gorges Dam is still being built, but its hydroelectric generator is expected to produce energy equivalent to 15 nuclear reactors.

EGYPT—Aswan Dam provides irrigation and electricity for the whole country.

CHINA—Coal makes up most of China's energy supply, with China both the largest consumer and largest producer of coal in the world.

AUSTRALIA AND NEW ZEALAND—Hydro and geothermal power stations supply 25 percent of electricity needs.

AFRICA

AUSTRALIA

Electricity Usage

- Very high
- Moderate
- Low
- Extremely low

ANTARCTICA

Activity

BITS AND PIECES: Start your own electricity scrapbook. What electrifying facts can you collect? You can use your scrapbook to tell the history of electricity. Or collect pictures of your favorite electrical inventions. Or just put in anything you get charged up about.

You're WIRED!

Electrons are in everything that exists, and that, of course, includes every cell of your body. Very, very small electric currents make your muscles move. And as in the circuits in your house, an overload of electricity—like an electrical shock or a lightning strike—can have dramatic effects.

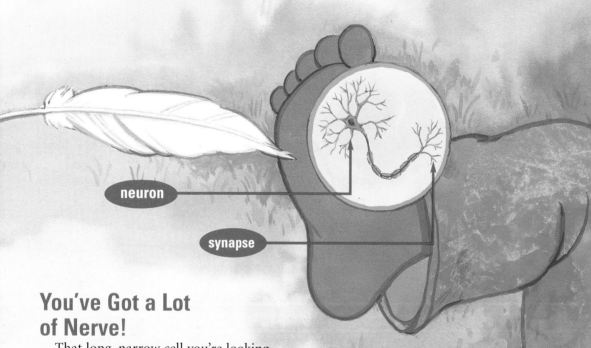

neuron

synapse

You've Got a Lot of Nerve!

That long, narrow cell you're looking at (above) is a nerve cell or neuron. There are about 100 billion neurons in your body. Most human nerve cells are less than 3 inches (7.6 cm) long, but the longest is about 3 feet (1 m) long. By comparison, the longest nerve cell in a whale is 30 feet (9 m) long.

Nerves send messages throughout your body. They do this with electric charges, which travel from one end of a nerve cell to another. But the current does not flow directly to the next neuron. There is a tiny gap between nerve cells called a synapse. Chemical messages released at the end of the nerve cell are picked up by the next one in line. So messages in your nervous system are sent by a combination of electrical and chemical signals.

Keeping the Beat

The heart has special groups of cells called pacemakers that control your heartbeat. A healthy heart at rest beats between 60 and 80 times per minute. But if you're excited or working hard, your heart rate can double.

An electrocardiograph machine (EKG) measures the strength and timing of the electric charges produced by the heart. If the heart's natural pacemaker cells stop sending out strong signals, an artificial pacemaker can help do the job. These devices are connected to the heart with wires and run on batteries.

pacemaker cells

The Shock That Saves

Some people with heart trouble need a shock of electricity to "reset" their heartbeats. In these cases, heart muscles have become disorganized. Instead of beating together strongly, the muscles twitch weakly. This is called fibrillation. An electric shock will stop the heart briefly and allow the muscles to regain their rhythm. When you see doctors on TV giving a patient a shock, that's what they're doing.

Too Much of a Good Thing

Even though electricity is a natural part of you, too much of it can kill you. How much is too much? An electric chair uses about 2,000 volts at 5 amperes. It is a strong enough current to stop the heart from beating.

A large current will also cause muscles to contract. A person touching a live wire may not be able to let go. If you ever see someone getting a shock, be careful not to touch him or her. Get help and have the current turned off.

Being struck by lightning can kill you. But some people have been hit by lightning more than once and lived.

Activity

NERVOUS REACTION: How is a nerve cell like a battery? Write and draw an advertisement for "Nerve Batteries." Make up a brand name for them. Explain why someone would buy them.

Eel-ectricity

A ray's prey is in for a shock.

All animals produce electricity in their bodies, but some produce a lot more than others. And that can come as a nasty shock for other animals in the area.

The South American electric eel even has an electric-sounding scientific name—*Electrophorus electricus.* This fish has special cells in its tail that can produce around six hundred volts of electricity—more than the current in your house. The total amount of electricity it creates isn't enough to kill an adult human being, but it is enough to stun or kill the small fish the eel eats. This natural talent makes up for something else: the eel has no teeth. A stunned fish is a lot easier to catch—and swallow.

Also, electric eels are nearly blind. But the waters where they live are dark, so sight wouldn't be very useful anyway. Instead of looking for supper, the eel uses its electric generating power to sense other fish. While swimming, it sends out low pulses of electricity that act like a sort of "radar."

Other kinds of fish are also electrically talented. A type of catfish in Africa can produce electric shocks with its special skin cells. In addition, an electric ray (also called the Atlantic torpedo) uses special large muscle cells on either side of its head to send out electric shocks.

Then there are sharks. They don't use electricity to kill, but they can sense electric currents from other animals. They have about one thousand electricity-sensing pits on either side of their heads. These can detect the tiny electric currents made by the muscles of other fish as they swim nearby.

A shark's electrical power is the "pits."

tricity

The electric eel has a stunning talent.

Certain catfish have special power built into their skin.

Activity

STUNNING CHANGES: All nerve and muscle cells generate small amounts of electricity. But electric eels have evolved with muscles that make enough current to stun other fish. Now those muscles aren't used as muscles anymore—they're used only to make electricity. Can you think of other animals that have body parts that have changed through evolution? How might these changes be similar to the electric muscles of the eel? How are they different? What conditions do you think caused them?

THE CASE OF THE Curious Circuit

"Someone has stolen the Electric Emerald!" announced E. Fields, electric detective. "And the crook is in this room!"

The four suspects all began to talk at once.

"Impossible!" shouted Professor Pulse.

"One of us?" Daphne Dynamo replied nervously.

"It wasn't me," said Bridget Battery.

"That's ridiculous!" exclaimed Charles Charge.

"No," Detective Field said slowly. "It isn't ridiculous. It had to be one of you. You were the

only ones in the house at the time of the robbery. Now, each of you please tell me what you were doing at 10:00 PM."

"I was drying my hair," Ms. Dynamo said quickly. "That's probably why I didn't hear anything."

Bridget Battery looked Field right in the eye. "I was playing my electric guitar," she stated. "And I had the volume way up."

"I'm afraid I was using my computer to get my e-mail," Professor Pulse told the group. "I must have been concentrating, because I didn't hear anything either."

"Well," Charles Charge said evenly. "I was just sitting in my room, playing a video game. It made a lot of noise and so did that old air conditioner."

Field thought for a moment. "Did you really have the air conditioner on?" he asked Mr. Charge.

"Yes," the man replied. "My room is still cool. You can go check if you want."

The detective did just that. When he returned a minute later, he made a dramatic announcement.

"Mr. Charge's room is cold," he told the group. "And after checking the wiring of this house, I found something unusual. All the rooms are on one circuit! And that means I can tell you who is lying. And that person is probably the thief who stole the emerald! It was Ms. Dynamo!"

How did the electric detective know it was Daphne Dynamo?

Clues

Reading lamp 100 watts
Guitar amplifier 120 watts
Computer monitor 110 watts
Computer 75 watts
Hair dryer 1200 watts
Television 90 watts
Video game player 12 watts
Air conditioner 750 watts
Light bulbs 75 watts each

All four rooms are on the same circuit.

The circuit contains 110 volts and 15 amps.

Be sure to check back on the almanac pages if you need to. (There's a hint in the illustration.)

(Answer on page 32)

BLACk

On the evening of November 9, 1965, thirty million people in the northeast United States found themselves suddenly without power. A large transformer had blown out upstate, and New York City's power was tapped to support an area of thousands of square miles. As a result, the whole city went dark. How did a powerful city respond to this emergency? Better than you might think.

From **Life Magazine,** *November 19, 1965*

It seemed to me that the blackout quite literally transformed the people of New York. In the crowded streets, businessmen, coats removed so that their light-colored shirts could be seen, became volunteer cops and directed traffic. Though the sidewalks were jammed, there was little of the rude jostling that is part of the normal midday walking New York. In the theatrically silver light of a perfect full moon (a must for all future power failures) people peered into the faces of passersby like children at a Halloween party trying to guess which friends hid behind which masks. In fact, the darkness made everyone more childlike. There was much laughter.

Quite suddenly 30 million people had to improvise. Walking down many flights of stairs, trudging across bridges, driving without the electronically imposed courtesy of stoplights, all these unusual things had to be done and people not only did them but carried them off with a certain splendid gaiety.

I was astounded to hear the saga of the five men trapped in an elevator 25 floors up in the Empire State Building who passed their 5¼ hours of black suspension by joking, singing and not panicking. When the lights came on the next morning, I saw a piece of television news which showed some people who'd been stuck all night in a subway car. A crowded mixed bag of young and old, well-dressed and shabby, they seemed absolutely overjoyed at their predicament. And when the subway policeman who'd been stuck with them congratulated them on the way they had been good comrades and otherwise passed the time courageously, they cheered him wildly.

Loudon Wainwright

OuT!

It was a chilly November night. I was 15, and had just come home from Brooklyn Technical High School. It was dark already, because Daylight Savings Time a week or so earlier had made us "fall back" an hour. But there was a big bright moon.

I was just settling down to eat dinner when the lights dimmed, the TV screen shrank. Then they returned to normal.

"Hey Mom," I called, " Are you using the electric broiler that always blows the fuse again?"

Then the lights "browned out" again—but in a second they went out completely!

When we determined it wasn't a blown fuse, we lit candles and turned on a battery-powered radio and heard the news.

Over the next several hours, the 3 generations of my family gathered around that radio in a close, and even happy way—a way we had never done before. I forgot my first lesson in how dependent on electricity our modern lives had become—gas stations couldn't pump gas, people had to control the traffic

since the stoplights were out. Everything I took for granted, like the TV that was always on since the day I was born—could just grind to a halt and go dark. I was glad I wasn't stuck in the subway like thousands of commuters. I was glad I was home with my family.

The lights came back about 12 hours later, but though I'm middle-aged now, I never forgot the excitement of that November night when the lights went out.

Ed Strnad, The Blackout Project
sloan.stanford.edu./blackout

Activity

THE DARK SIDE: Twelve years later, in the summer of 1977, the New York metropolitan region experienced another massive power outage, but this time the response was different. There were riots and looting, which inflicted enormous economic damage. Do some research on the economic and social conditions at the time. Why were the responses to the same crisis so different? Use the library and electricity-related Web sites for research. What would your town be like in a total blackout?

RISKY BUSINESS
A Life on the Line

How do you work on a wire that carries 500,000 volts? Very carefully. How carefully? Ask George Wragg.

George has been working for New Jersey's Public Service Electricity and Gas Company for forty-three years. He's worked on all sorts of wires, from the ones that bring power to single-family homes to the ones strung along steel towers 300 feet (91 m) tall. Those wires have current charged with 138 kilovolts to 500 kilovolts. That's hundreds of thousands of volts. And the amperage is also very high. How does he stay safe?

"We prefer to work on lines in a de-energized state," he explains. "Dead lines." So the first thing to do is try to turn off the power. But sometimes, a line can't be turned off, because it would cut power to an area. Then the repair crews have to work on "live" lines.

"We often have to replace insulators or other hardware," George says. "They get hit by lightning strikes or just wear out." Insulators hold the wires on the tower and are made of porcelain or some other nonconducting material.

TOWER OF STRENGTH

To get to the lines, you have to climb the tower. A transmission tower can be anywhere from sixty to 300 feet (91 m) tall.

"Each tower has a climbing leg," George explains. "In that leg of the tower are steps. When I first climbed one, I had already been working on tall poles, so it wasn't too bad. But if you're new, it takes some getting used to."

At the top of the steps, the line worker uses a ladder to reach the wire and the part that has to be replaced. The wire is bare metal, and it's charged with hundreds of thousands of volts. But the workers can touch the line and survive—if they do it the right way. The trick is not to be *grounded*. That means that electricity can't flow from the wire through you into something else.

"As long as you're not grounded," George says, "the current will flow around you. It's like you become part of the wire. That's why birds can roost on those wires. You have to isolate yourself with some kind of insulation." To make sure this happens, the ladders that the repair persons stand on are insulated. The workers also use other equipment to keep safe. Everyone wears a safety harness to prevent falls. And everyone wears a special suit made out of fireproof material and metal threads. The metal threads conduct electricity. But is that good? Yes. It conducts the electricity away from the body.

MAGIC WAND

When the tower worker first goes near the wire, he uses a wand or metal rod. The wand is attached to his suit. He touches the wire with the wand first to conduct the electricity to the suit. Now the suit is carrying the same voltage as the wire, and the lineman can go to work.

It's risky business, all right, and not many people are authorized to do it. Tower workers have to go through a seven-year apprenticeship. First they learn how to climb the tower. Then they move on to working with dead wires. Finally, they work on live lines. But even with all their safety precautions, unexpected things can happen on a high voltage wire.

"We try to be aware of lightning storms in the area," George says. "But a storm might be forty miles away and we wouldn't know about it." If lightning strikes a power line even forty miles from where the repair work is being done, a surge of electricity will run through the line.

"One time we were on a tower, and lightning struck the line we were working on. It made a loud, rumbling sound like a freight train as it whooshed by. There was a lot of scrambling on that tower."

But as George Wragg tells it, the tower workers don't focus on the danger in their jobs. Instead, they get a lot of pride and satisfaction from it.

"You get sort of a freedom when you work on top of the tower," he says. "You're your own boss, and your destiny depends on yourself. The people who do this work take a great pride in it. There aren't a lot of people in the nation who can do it."

But that doesn't mean they aren't careful every time they go up. "You still have to watch that current," George warns. "It wants to leap out and bite you."

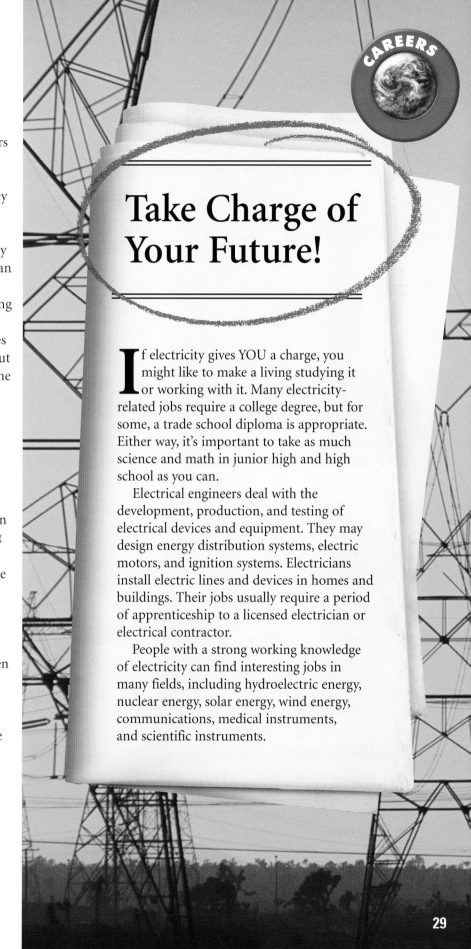

CAREERS

Take Charge of Your Future!

If electricity gives YOU a charge, you might like to make a living studying it or working with it. Many electricity-related jobs require a college degree, but for some, a trade school diploma is appropriate. Either way, it's important to take as much science and math in junior high and high school as you can.

Electrical engineers deal with the development, production, and testing of electrical devices and equipment. They may design energy distribution systems, electric motors, and ignition systems. Electricians install electric lines and devices in homes and buildings. Their jobs usually require a period of apprenticeship to a licensed electrician or electrical contractor.

People with a strong working knowledge of electricity can find interesting jobs in many fields, including hydroelectric energy, nuclear energy, solar energy, wind energy, communications, medical instruments, and scientific instruments.

Catch a

Morse Code

A ._	J .___	S ...	2 .._ _ _
B _...	K _._	T _	3 ..._ _
C _._.	L ._..	U .._	4 ...._
D _..	M _ _	V ..._	5 .....
E .	N _.	W ._ _	6 _....
F .._.	O _ _ _	X _.._	7 _ _...
G _ _.	P ._ _.	Y _._ _	8 _ _ _..
H	Q _ _._	Z _ _..	9 _ _ _ _.
I ..	R ._.	1 ._ _ _ _	0 _ _ _ _ _

You may play a game called "telephone," in which players sit in a circle and a whispered message is passed around the room. How about a game of telegraph?

To play, you'll need two teams of two people each. Each team writes down four short messages (no more than three or four words). Put the messages in a hat or some other container. One person is the "sender." He or she picks a message and has to tap it out in Morse Code for the "receiver." Then the receiver has to write out the message. Alternate between teams and let each team member take a turn as a "sender." See which team is better at sending and understanding Morse Code.

Samuel Morse was not the first person to build a telegraph machine. In fact, when he thought up the idea for a telegraph machine, he was disappointed to learn that someone had already invented it! But he was the first to come up with a simple code for sending messages over a wire. Now that you have the Morse Code, you can use it to send messages yourself—and you don't need a telegraph.

To write a word, leave a space between the code for each letter. For example, to write CAT in Morse code you would write

_ . _ .   . _   _

To write a sentence, leave a bigger space between each word.

The first telegraph machines printed the dots and dashes on paper. But telegraph operators soon learned to understand the code from the clicks the machine made. You can send Morse Code messages by tapping on a desk or banging on a drum.

Code

A SHOCKING CURE

In 1780, doctors in London begin seeing patients who believe they are paralyzed. The doctors can find nothing wrong with these people. But they do come up with a cure. They give the people electric shocks that make their muscles jump. Once the patients see this, they stop believing they are paralyzed and are "cured."

Boston, MA, 1868

Thomas Edison, working at a telegraph office early in his career, has a big problem. Make that, a bug problem. In his own words:

The office was on the ground floor and had, previous to occupation by the Telegraph Co., been a restaurant. It was literally loaded with cockroaches, who lived between the wall and the board running around the room at the floor. These were such a bother on my table that I pasted two strips of tinfoil on the wall at my desk, connecting one piece to the positive pole of the big battery supplying current to the wires and the negative pole to the other strip. The cockroaches moving up on the wall would pass over the strips, and the moment they got their legs across both strips, there was a flash of light and the cockroach went into gas. This automatic electrocution device attracted so much attention and got a one-half column description in an evening paper, that the Manager made me stop it.

Ethiopia (then Abyssinia), 1890

EMPEROR MENLIK II orders three electric chairs to be delivered to his kingdom, forgetting one important detail—there is no electric power in his country. His plans for modern executions have to be put on hold. But the purchase isn't a total waste—he makes one of the electric chairs into his new throne!

Good as New

Four-year-old Ashley Perry was born without a complete left hand. But now she has a new one—one that's powered by a tiny motor and rechargeable batteries. Ashley operates the hand by moving different groups of muscles in her upper arm. Electrodes on her arm measure the movements and send signals to the motors in her *myoelectric* hand. (*Myo* means muscle in Greek). With her new hand, Ashley can do almost everything other kids can do.

A Real-Life Frankenstein

In 1818, the same year Mary Shelley publishes her novel *Frankenstein*, Dr. Andrew Ure publicly electrifies a human corpse. He attaches electrodes to a major nerve, causing the corpse to shake. As other nerves become stimulated, the corpse seems to breathe, sigh, smile, and frown. Most of the world has barely heard of electricity at the time. This demonstration leaves people wondering if the strange new power can really bring humans back from the dead.

YOUR WORLD YOUR TURN

Final Project:
Lose the Juice

It's a big project. But when you're done, you might have come up with real ways to save your school money and save some of the world's resources too.

Look around your school. How many things do you see that use electricity? Electric lights, clocks, pencil sharpeners? Do you know where the electricity comes from? Do you know how it is produced?

Suppose the long power lines that carry electricity to your school suddenly vanished. What would you do? Could you figure out ways to make your school run? Where would you get electricity?

Here's what you have to do:

1 Form a team of four or five students to work on the problem. Your first job is to figure out how much electric power your school uses now. You'll have to conduct a survey of all the electrical devices in your school. How many watts do they use when they are running? (Most appliances have that information written on them somewhere.) How many hours or minutes per day are they on? You want to find out the total number of watts your school uses on an average day.

2 Then you have to think about other sources of power. Do you want to find out about solar panels? Portable generators? What about batteries? Or a generator that runs by wind power? How much power can each source supply? How much would it cost to buy? How much would it cost to run? How does that compare with the cost of electricity from your local power company?

3 How about energy conservation? Are there ways your school can cut down on electricity use? Should you? Could you use fewer electric appliances or ones that use less energy? Exactly how much electricity could you save? Could you save money that way?

4 Finally, make a report to the class. You should list all the sources of electricity you plan to use, how much power each source will generate, and how much it will cost per watt. Would it be practical to generate power yourselves? Would it make more sense to generate some of the power yourself and buy the rest from the power company?

Two places to look for information are your local power company and the U.S. Department of Energy (www.eia.doe.gov). You could also contact your school board or local government to find out how much they pay for electricity.

ANSWER
Solve-It-Yourself Mystery pages 24–25:

If Ms. Dynamo had really been drying her hair, the circuit would have been overloaded. A circuit breaker would have turned off the power to the house. Therefore, Detective Field knew she was lying and probably was the thief. (Clue in the illustration: She is washing, not drying, her hair.)